I Can Count Amazing Things

A Count and Word Book

By Pamela Cotton-Roberts, Ed.D

& Walter F. Cotton, Sr.

For parents and children everywhere, --PCR, & WFC

To order additional copies of this book, contact:
Xlibris
1-888-795-4274
www.Xlibris.com
Orders@Xlibris.com

1 Bubble Ball

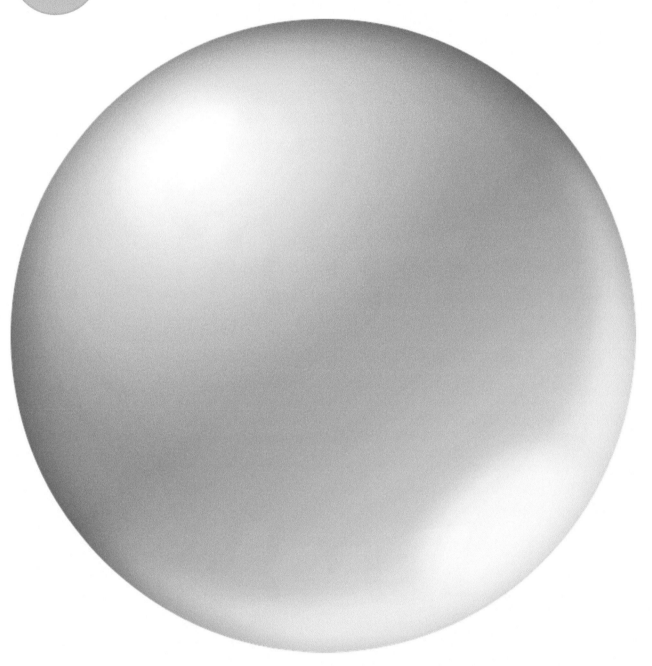

Green Grasshoppers

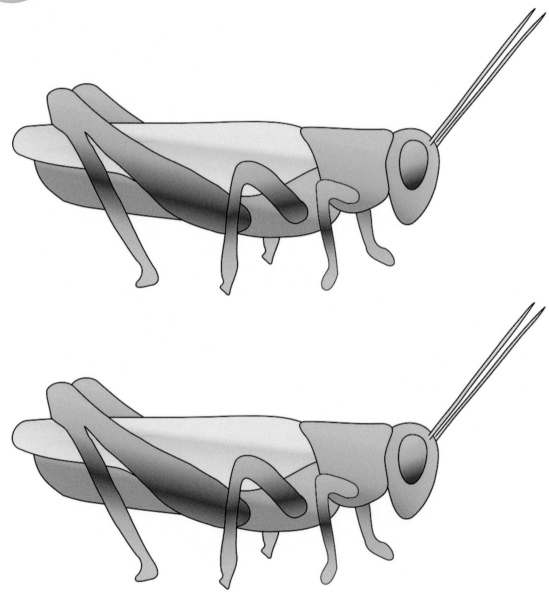

3 Courageous Cat

4 Large Ladybugs

5 Beautiful Butterflies

6 Adorable Ants

7 Busy Bees

8 Lucky Lizards

9 **Dotted Dogs**

10 Fresh Fish

12 Cozy Cows

13 Crazy Carrots

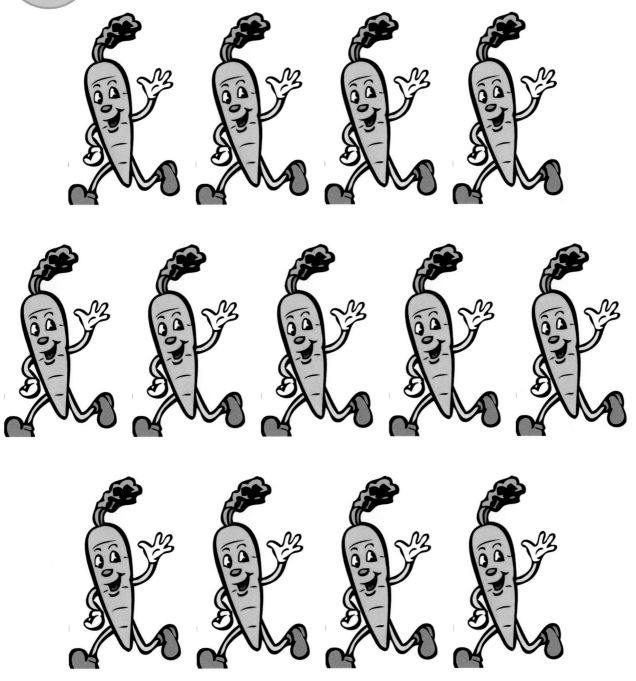

14 Unique Ukuleles

Zippy Zippers

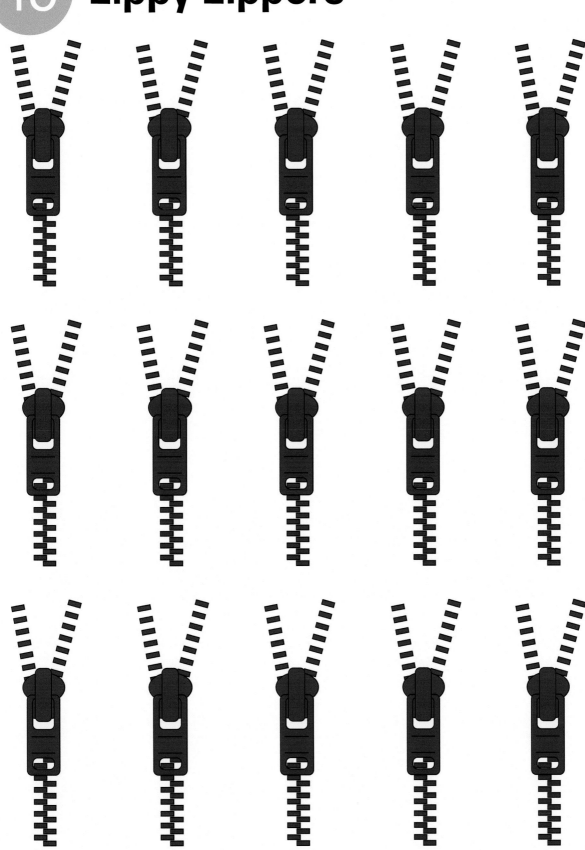

16 Wide Windows

Happy Hamsters

18 Fabulous Flamingos

19 Pink Pigs

 # Dashing Dragonflies

The Dragonfly

The dragonfly's eye consists of a tiny photoreception parts which means it can distinguish brightness and colors. The dragonfly can see in different directions. The dragonfly has the ability to detect fast movement.

The dragonfly is an amazing insect that can see large directions like this amazing counting and word book.

Printed in the United States
By Bookmasters